TABLE OF CONTENTS

Prologue 2

Disclaimer 3

Dedications 4

Note from the Author 5

Chapter 1 – Who Is an Entrepreneur? 6

Chapter 2 – Entrepreneurship or Servantship? 9

Chapter 3 – Initial Preparation 12

Chapter 4 – Mindset, Attitude and Approach 15

Chapter 5 – Build Meaningful Relations 18

Chapter 6 – Choose your Service Providers 21

Chapter 7 – Financial Framework 25

Chapter 8 – Formulation of Business Model 28

Chapter 9 – Compliances and Support Functions 31

Chapter 10 – Creating Brand Awareness 34

Chapter 11 – Recognize and Choose your Customer 37

Chapter 12 – The Conclusion 40

About the Author 43

Appendix 46

Prologue

Hearty congratulations on deciding to start your own venture! Thank you for expressing your willingness to know more about how you can proceed with your new undertaking. This book contains information gained from the personal experience of the author. The options outlined are based on personal research conducted.

This book is for salaried employees seeking to start their own business, new and established business owners, freelancers, students, aspiring and budding entrepreneurs, housewives looking to get back to earning. Others not mentioned here can still read this book. Maybe, they might get an idea or a set of ideas to become an entrepreneur.

Ideas can be conceived at any time anywhere. They key is to nurture it in the right way, with the right set of people in the right environment akin to a plant. With the right nurturing and fertilizer, it will flourish and bear fruit. The sweetness of the fruit will depend on the level of patience of the caretaker. Generally, a good gardener has a high level of patience, perseverance and endurance.

Disclaimer

Copyright © 2019 by Ayaz Zanzeria. All rights reserved worldwide. This is not a free publication. No part of this publication may be replicated, redistributed, or given away in any form without the prior written consent of the author/publisher or the terms relayed to you herein. This publication is designed to provide accurate and authoritative information about the subject matter covered. The contents of this book are based on the author's experience, original ideas and concepts. None of these have been copied from any other source. If there is a match between any part of this book and the other source, it could be either the author has given consent for his work to be published or it is a coincidence, or it has been copied without the author's knowledge.

This publication is sold in the understanding that the publisher is not engaged in rendering legal, accounting, or other professional services. If legal advice or other expert assistance is required, the services of a legal or professional should be sought. Thanks!

Dedications

This book is dedicated to my loving mother and my beloved wife who have always stood by me, through thick and thin, through adversity and prosperity, happiness and sadness, through quarrels and re-unions, etc.

Credits to my schoolteachers and school mates who have grown with me with teaching, learning, funning, punning, fighting, uniting, playing, competing, etc.

Credits to all the people around me who have stood by me through thick and thin, physically or mentally, personally or virtually, on or off social media, tenured or youngsters, etc.

Last but not the least, credits to the reader and writer, hunter and hunted, agents and supervisors, team leaders and managers, colleagues, peers and teammates, friends and acquaintances, online and offline, etc., to provide such inspiring stories and incidents for me to pen them into a book. You may or may not have served me directly or indirectly, but now it's payback time from you to me via me authoring and monetizing this book. 😊

Note from the Author

Dear Reader,

My solemn gratitude to you for taking the time to read this book. The reason why you are reading this book is because you have accepted that it is not easy to be an entrepreneur. Yes, it is always good to get some guidance and tips on how to get started. I have attempted to list down the various challenges and how to overcome them in this book.

This entire book is based purely on my personal experience that I have lived during my journey as an entrepreneur. I trust this book will give you some good insights and tips on how you can move forward with your venture.

Entrepreneurship is a lifestyle that needs to be embraced. It is a state of mind and a thought process. Wish you all the very best with your venture. May God grant you success and courage with your endeavour.

Yours truly,

Ayaz Shabbir Zanzeria

Chapter 1 – Who Is an Entrepreneur?

Introduction

Who is an entrepreneur? A person who embarks on a journey of trading goods or services for making a profit while taking risks. This requires a positive mindset with a business acumen and the ability to be prepared to meet all ups and downs at every time. Not everybody who has an idea can become an entrepreneur. There is a difference between a successful entrepreneur and a sustainable entrepreneur. In this series of articles, I will attempt to highlight the major differences between the two based on personal experiences of self and with others.

Sustainable Entrepreneur – Prelude

What is sustainability? This is a state of "equilibrium" in which progress is made at a steady and maintainable rate. Which then brings us to, who is a sustainable entrepreneur or what is sustainable entrepreneurship? Simply put, an entrepreneur who defines his rate of growth in a way that he is making consistent and sustainable progress in his journey of creating wealth.

Successful Entrepreneur – Prelude

What is the meaning of success? Different people have different definitions and meanings for success. One of the most popular meanings is to associate success with loads of money and fame. Who is a successful entrepreneur or what is successful entrepreneurship? A person who has made a lot of money in a short span of time.

Getting Started

Now that we have understood the different types of entrepreneurship meanings and definitions, the tricky question to think about is, "which of these would you like to be, a sustainable entrepreneur or a successful one?" Once you are clear in your mind, then the next thing to think about is, what is your passion? What are you good at? What are your skills? It could be anything like drawing, artwork, writing, sewing, cooking, singing, dancing, acting, directing, stand-up comedy etc. There are plenty of options to choose from.

The key question to consider is, which of your skills defines you, which you can take forward to consistently create wealth for you.

After identifying your core skills, take your time to create a few initial works. This will help you polish and formulate your way of doing things. Share your initial creations with your immediate friends and family members and get an opinion and feedback. This will be a "dipstick" test for your concept or idea. From this set of people, you will get both – positive and negative feedback. Take both in a very positive way. Do not get discouraged by the negative feedback even if it comes in the form of criticism. Channelize your feeling of vengeance to fuel your passion to do better and silence your critics.

Synopsis

To summarize, do a little bit of groundwork or preparation to begin your entrepreneurship journey. This is analogous to preparing for a road trip. Plan your trip well, however, also plan for and be prepared for the sudden breaks and contingencies that you may come across. This is the initial stage. Thank you for reading this. In the subsequent chapters, I will talk about taking the next step in moving forward.

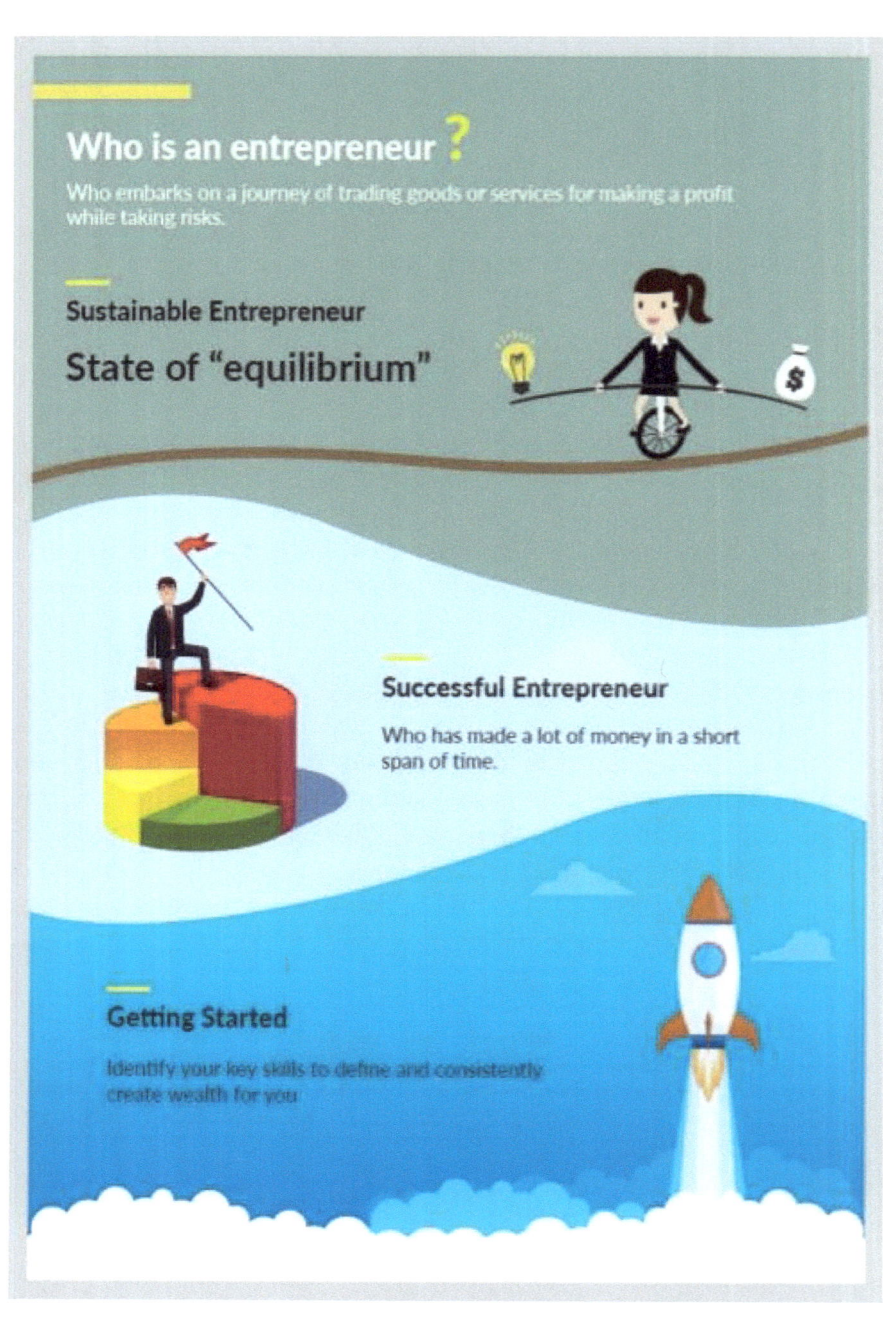

Chapter 2 – Entrepreneurship or Servantship?

Introduction

In the first chapter, we read about a successful and a sustainable entrepreneur. We also understood who an entrepreneur is. In a nutshell, entrepreneurship is not just about making money, rather it's about building your capacity to take risks to reap in monetary and other rewards.

Career Options

Everybody can embark on an entrepreneurship journey, however some become successful while some become sustainable, some fail, and some go on to start multiple businesses and call themselves as "serial entrepreneurs".

Some are of the mindset that they can study courses, get accolades and certificates, which will help them get high paying jobs. That is not entirely true. Hence the need to properly evaluate the options with data and in a systematic way to make an informed decision.

The Decision-Making Process

For many, the first thing that is taught to us is to study to take up a job. Is that really what all of us want to do? For some, yes... for the others, no. For aspiring entrepreneurs, some initial groundwork needs to be done. Consider the below questions:

1) What is your passion?
2) What product and/or service are you looking to offer?
3) What makes your offering special?
4) What problem are you solving?
5) Have you shared your concept with your friends and family?
6) What is the initial feedback?
7) Do you have faith in your offering and it's potential?

8) Do you have any family members or friends who are willing to support you unconditionally to take your concept forward?

Once you have answers to most of these questions, it becomes easy to a large extent. These questions are not an exhaustive or an exclusive list. These have been compiled based on personal experience.

Considerations

What you also need to contemplate on are the pros and cons of a job. Draw a comparison between being salaried versus being a business owner. Each have their own merits and demerits. Additional questions to mull over are:
- What are you interested in?
- What is your passion?
- What is your dream?
- Do you want to be a successful employee?
- Do you want to become a sustainable entrepreneur?

One good approach would be to list a comparison chart on a whiteboard – job versus entrepreneurship. This will give a clear picture of the career options by weighing the pros and cons of both. Take the help of family and friends for the brainstorming session. Apart from the above, they may add additional points that may have been overlooked.

A word of caution: it is good to take advice, suggestions and recommendations from near and dear ones. Do not blindly trust anyone nor take anyone's word based on sheer experience. Do additional research on that aspect before arriving to any decision.

Synopsis

To conclude, you need to weigh the pros and cons of entrepreneurship versus "servantship". For the former, you further need to weigh the responses to the questions mentioned above. Take your time. Just make an informed decision. Thank you for reading the second chapter.

> **Entrepreneurship is about building your capacity to take risks to reap in monetary and other rewards.**

Career Options

"employed or self-employed"

properly evaluate the options with data and in a systematic way to make an informed decision

The Decision-Making Process

1) What is your passion?
2) What product and/or service are you looking to offer?
3) What makes your offering special?
4) What problem are you solving?
5) Have you shared your concept with your friends and family?
6) What is the initial feedback?
7) Do you have faith in your offering and it's potential?
8) Do you have any family members or friends who are willing to support you unconditionally to take your concept forward?

Considerations

Draw a comparison between being salaried versus being a business owner.

Chapter 3 – Initial Preparation

Introduction

Thank you for reading the previous two chapters of this book. The initial chapters consist of a list of questions that need to be asked and considered. These will help in painting a holistic picture of entrepreneurship. These will serve as a guide to help you monetize your concept in a structured manner.

Entrepreneurship is just not about monetizing your concept or skillset. It's about doing it the efficient way which is legally compliant with fair and ethical business practices.

Preparing the Journey

We have seen the contemplations that need to be mulled over to arrive at a consensus with yourself. Once that is done, then prepare for the next step with the help of this checklist:

- What will be the brand name?
- What will be the name of the legal entity?
- What will be the type of legal entity (private limited (Pvt Ltd), public limited (Ltd), one-person company (OPC), sole-proprietorship, limited liability partnership (LLP), freelance, etc.
- How many members will be involved initially as the core team?
- What will be the amount of initial investment?
- Who will do the initial investment?
- How will you take care of company accounts?
- How do you plan to grow and expand your reach?
- Which activities will you outsource?
- Which activities will you handle yourself?

This is not an exhaustive or exclusive list. However, you can take this as a starting point to help you give direction and focus to your core concept. Do reach out to practicing Chartered Accountants (CAs) and Company

Secretaries (CS). Most of them are friendly and do offer valuable advice and guidance in the form of free consultation. They will guide you in terms of best practices followed in the industry and in terms of compliance norms to be implemented and maintained. They are the best guides as they work with different companies in different domains, hence their experience is varied.

Each of these points require careful thought and planning with proper paperwork in place. After the thoughts and brainstorming has been done, then all the above points need to be implemented or put in action, one by one. A word of caution, especially for the investments part – ensure proper and complete paperwork. Its not just about getting the money to get started, however, do ensure that proper agreements are executed, appropriately signed with adequate witnesses. This is for the safety and surety of both – the entrepreneur and the investor. A practicing Company Secretary (CS) or a Corporate Lawyer would be the best guide to help you with this.

Synopsis

The initial preparation for beginning the entrepreneurship journey is exhaustive but to ensure that the building is steady, its foundation must be strong. Entrepreneurship is a journey of endurance and perseverance. The journey of a salaried individual is tough; however, it is comparatively simpler as it does not require all-round skills that are needed by an entrepreneur.

Thank you for continuing reading and staying with me in this journey. Hope that these points are valuable for you especially for budding and aspiring entrepreneurs. For those already into entrepreneurship for quite some time, hope you find something in these that you may have overlooked which you can still implement in your existing ventures.

Entrepreneurship is about monetizing your concept or skillset.

business practices

Preparing the Journey
prepare

- ★ What will be the brand name?
- ★ What will be the name of the legal entity?
- ★ What will be the type of legal entity (private limited (Pvt Ltd), public limited (Ltd), one-person company (OPC), sole-proprietorship, partnership, limited liability partnership (LLP), freelance, etc.
- ★ How many members will be involved initially as the core or founder team?
- ★ What will be the amount of initial investment?
- ★ Who will do the initial investment?
- ★ How will you take care of company accounts?
- ★ How do you plan to grow and expand your reach?
- ★ Which activities will you outsource?
- ★ Which activities will you handle yourself?

brainstorming

Each of these points require careful thought and planning with proper paperwork in place.

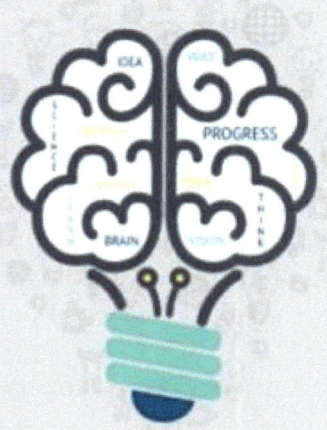

Chapter 4 – Mindset, Attitude and Approach

Introduction

Thank you for reaching this far with the entrepreneurship journey. In this chapter, we are going to focus on an important aspect of entrepreneurship – mindset and attitude. These are critical in helping you scale. The direction, upwards or downwards, will be decided on your own approach. This chapter will simply lay down some do's and don'ts with the possible consequences and impacts.

Positive Mindset and Attitude

With a positive attitude, an individual always looks for opportunities in every difficulty. He even accepts the fact that his business partner and he have varying thought processes and business ideologies. He will always look to keep a balance without offending his partner's sentiments and business acumen.

With this attitude, an entrepreneur will always be solution-focused in every discussion, he will be more people-centric and empathetic. He will be down-to-earth and will also value his own and others' self-respect.

Negative Mindset and Attitude

With a negative approach, the individual cannot differentiate between "what is right" and "I am right". He will always look to have "my way or the highway". His ego will be higher than the sky which will get hurt often, especially when he hears words like "no", "it's not possible", "it can't be done". This will cause more violent reactions than calm positive responses.

With this approach, he will not listen to reason, even if it is legally binding. Such entrepreneurs will pose unnecessary challenges without proper justification. This attitude and approach will cause more harm than good. All his potential clients, partners and associates will always look to avoid him as he does not value or respect other people. Such type of entrepreneurs tends to be selfish and haughtily arrogant.

Consequences and Impact

Entrepreneurs with a negative mindset or an arrogant attitude will only make enemies. Their task will only be uphill in all aspects – getting clients, partners, forming meaningful business relations, maintaining employees, etc.

On the other hand, an entrepreneur with a down-to-earth approach towards people, will be more careful in maintaining relations with all business partners and associates. Clients will refer him to friends and family.

Synopsis

It is pertinent to develop and maintain a balanced attitude. This will go a long way in maintaining fruitful and mutually beneficial relations with your clients, vendors, employees, partners, associates, freelancers and whoever you develop business relations with. It is important to identify and build relations that will help build brand value in the long run.

Entrepreneurs with a humble approach and down-to-earth attitude will go on to become sustainable entrepreneurs. In the entrepreneurship journey, there will be ups and downs which need an attitude of endurance and perseverance. Thank you for reading this part as well. In the next chapter I will share more on my personal experience of my entrepreneurship journey.

Entrepreneurship – mindset and attitude

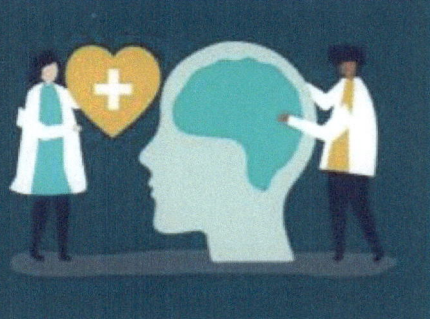

Positive Mindset and Attitude

With this attitude, an entrepreneur will always be solution-focused in every discussion

Negative Mindset and Attitude

will pose unnecessary challenges without proper justification

Consequences and Impact

Entrepreneurs with a negative mindset or an arrogant attitude will only make enemies.

an entrepreneur with a down-to-earth approach towards people, will be more careful in maintaining relations with all business partners and associates.

Chapter 5 – Build Meaningful Relations

Introduction

Thank you for reading the previous chapter of the entrepreneurship journey. In this chapter, we are going to focus on another important aspect of entrepreneurship – building meaningful relationships. These are critical in helping you expand your reach via recommendations. This chapter will outline a few aspects of building "ties that scale".

Relationship building starts the moment you decide to start your entrepreneurship journey. You need not wait for your company registration to complete. You need not wait for the legal formalities to be completed. The right time is NOW! Start building meaningful relationships at the earliest possible. You will be surprised to how far you can go once people start recommending you, your products and services over your competitors. This works more powerful than conventional and modern marketing techniques and campaigns.

Network to Build Relationships

Keep an eye out for the various meetup events happening at different venues. Ensure that you have ample visiting cards printed. Attend each event with at least 40-50 (on an average) visiting cards in your pocket. The number of attendees, type of organizers, the event venue and other factors will give you a fair idea of the number of people expected at the event. Utilize the time before the event start, coffee breaks and post event completion to network with the participants, exchange visiting cards and have a meaningful conversation about their businesses.

Be careful to have a conversation in which you are only creating awareness about your business, products and services. Attempts to be made to not sell anything to anyone. Simply focus on having the initial ice-breaker conversation. From their reaction and response, you will be able to gauge who is your potential customer. Here you will be able to easily filter your target audience for subsequent collaborators and follow ups.

Post the event, send a follow up email to all the people whom you have met and exchanged email addresses with. Keep the email short and brief with a link to your website, youtube channels or other online works of art. Avoid using images and attachments to make the email heavy. A simple text email will suffice as long as it is well worded and adequately spaced. This will remain on the records for the recipient. For this, you can use the online tools that are available for sending bulk emails.

From the visiting cards, you will have the contact numbers and names of the business owners, founders, co-founders, partners, marketing heads, directors, etc. Follow up with them occasionally with a semi-formal conversational phone call. They will entertain you in this approach. Be careful to not harass or bombard them with too much information as it can have negative impacts.

Synopsis

It is very important to keep the following points in mind.

- Master the art of "sell without selling".
- Learn to share your products/services with passion.
- Attempt to build long lasting personal relationships.
- Be a part of as many networks as possible on different social media platforms, offline and online.
- Gauge the audience and pitch accordingly.

Build meaningful relationships that will go a long way and not just for business. You never know who will refer you or reach out to you at what point of time for your services.

Chapter 6 – Choose your Service Providers

Introduction

Thank you for reading the previous chapters of the entrepreneurship journey. In this chapter, we are going to focus on the selection process. It could be any type of selection – selecting a vendor to service different business needs like a company secretary, accountant, auditor, technical team, marketing agency, banking partner, investor, employees, etc.

Identification

Google search will yield hundreds of results for any service provider. One tried and tested approach would be to meet people via references and prepare a list of the various services with the features and benefits with their respective offerings. For a given service provider, the services would be similar, however the offerings would vary. Make a comparison list between at least three service providers to get a holistic view. In doing so, the price would be one of the factors for consideration versus the only factor for consideration. The real question that needs to be answered is, "Is cheap really cheap?"

Comparison Chart

Illustrated below is a comparison chart that I had prepared in April 2017 when I had to select a payment gateway for one of my clients. The descriptions would vary as per the product and/or service as per the vendor or provider. The point is to make a properly informed decision after carefully considering various factors involved including quality of product and/or service, reviews, etc.

The parameters can be formulated based on the various requirements and the products and/or services can be mapped accordingly. Different parameters can be categorised and then grouped together. These will give a "sub-rank" in each category. Subsequently, all of these can be clubbed together to give an overall ranking.

Parameters	Importance	Citrus/PayUMoney Feature	Weight	Score	RazorPay Feature	Weight	Score	Instamojo Feature	Weight	Score
Security										
SSL Encryption	9	Yes - 128 bit	9	81	Yes	9	81	Yes - 128 bit	9	81
2FA	9	Yes	9	81	Yes	9	81	Yes	9	81
Compliance Standard	9	ISO 27001:2013	9	81	Not ISO 27001:2013	3	27	Not ISO 27001:2013	3	27
PCI-DSS	9	Yes	9	81	Yes	9	81	Yes	9	81
Subtotal				324			270			270
Sub Rank				1			4			4
Payment Options										
Debit/Credit Cards	9	Yes	9	81	Yes	9	81	Yes	9	81
Intl Debit/Credit Cards	5	No	5	25	Yes	9	45	Yes	9	45
EMI	8	No	5	40	Yes	9	72	Yes	9	72
Net Banking	9	Yes	9	81	Yes	9	81	Yes	9	81
Mobile Wallets	5	No	5	25	Yes	8	40	Yes	8	40
UPI	9	Yes	8	72	Yes	8	72	Yes	8	72
Aadhaar Pay	7	No	4	28	No	4	28	No	4	28
Swipe Machine for POS	8	No	4	32	Yes	9	72	No	4	32
Social media payments	5	No	4	20	No	4	20	Yes	5	25
International Currencies	5	No	5	25	No	5	25	No	5	25
Subtotal				429			536			501
Sub Rank				6			3			5
Cost										
Setup Cost	8	No Cost	9	72	No Cost	9	72	No Cost	9	72
Annual Fee	8	No Cost	9	72	No Cost	9	72	No Cost	9	72
Transaction Fee	9	2% flat (1% add for	7	63	2% flat (3% flat for	7	63	2% + Rs 3 per trans	6	54
Subtotal				207			207			198
Sub Rank				2			2			4
Score				969			1022			982
Overall Rank				6			4			5

Considerations

Thus, this type of comparison chart helps to make a holistic comparison of products and/or services with similar features and offerings. This also helps to answer the question, "What value for money do we get?" On some occasions, if you are unsure of what you are looking for, enlisting the features in a comparison chart like this, also helps gain more clarity.

Another way to look at this, if you have a specific set of requirements in mind, these can be listed as parameters as per their categories. There will be additional features that will fall outside the purview of the initial requirements; however, these can be used as add-ons for comparison.

This type of chart does not have to be too complex, rather, it is a simple listing with simplified formulae. This is very useful for the below factors:

> ➢ Making an informed decision for selecting from a set of products and/or services.

- ➢ Choosing a vendor or service provider.
- ➢ For your own product or service, you can draw a comparison chart for your competitors' offerings and see where and how you can make a difference.

Synopsis

Selection is an important aspect and should follow a proper comparison process rather than simply looking at a single aspect or a small set of features. An overall comparison would give a 360-degree view and helps to make a better-informed decision. A similar approach can be taken for your products/services against your competitors to strategize your offerings to have the leading edge.

selection

selection process - selecting a vendor to service different business needs like a company secretary, accountant, auditor, technical team, marketing agency, banking partner, investor, employees, etc.

Identification

Make a comparison list between at least three service providers to get a holistic view.

Comparison Chart

make a properly informed decision after carefully considering various factors involved including quality of product and/or service, reviews, etc.

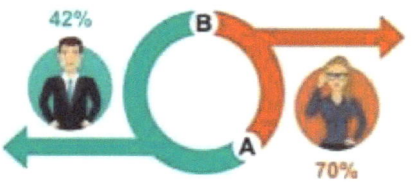

Considerations

What value for money do we get?

Specific set of requirements additional features that will fall outside the purview of the initial requirements, competitors' offerings

Chapter 7 – Financial Framework

Introduction

Thank you for reading the previous chapters of the entrepreneurship journey. In this chapter, we are going to focus on the core framework of the business – the financial system. This can be divided into three parts – the banking, the accounting system and the resource to manage this. Let's look at these aspects one by one.

Banking

There are plenty of banks that offer banking solutions for your business. Refer to the previous volume for the comparison chart to carefully examine the service offerings. Below are some of the points to be considered while selecting a banking partner:

- What are the features and benefits of the product?
- What is the schedule of charges for this product?
- What is the minimum balance that I will have to maintain?
- What facilities will I get and what will be the charges for each?
- What additional perks or offers will I get?
- Will there be a dedicated relationship manager?
- In case of issues, how will the issue resolution process work and what will be the turnaround time for this?
- Will I be able to receive foreign remittances in my account? If yes, what is the procedure to enable it?
- What will be the turnaround time for queries to be responded to?

Accounting System

The accounting system is a critical aspect and the backbone of any business. Every penny and transaction must be recorded. Hence, an accounting system should have the below features:

- Should be secure, tamper proof, strong data integrity and compliant as per international standards.
- Should be accessible from anywhere on any device.
- Manage all your expenses, revenues, customers, users, salespersons, vendors, invoices, receipts, taxes, compliances, bank accounts, etc. all under one roof.
- Generate various types of financial reports – standard and customized.

Resource

Resources primarily include accountants and auditors who manage the financial system. The accountants ensure that the books are maintained with proper copies of the invoices and receipts. Every year, auditors go through the books of accounts, spot and clarify any discrepancies, help rectify any defects and then prepare the financial statements (balance sheet, profit and loss statement, cash flow statement, statement of retained earnings and others as applicable) along with an audit report that needs to be submitted to the registrar of companies as part of annual compliance filing. It is imperative that the financials are compliant for the auditors to give a positive report or a clean chit. Hence, it is important to listen to the auditor as he will guide you with:

- Best practices for maintaining book of accounts.
- Ways and means to financially strategize revenue growth.
- Growth path for sustained revenue generation.

Synopsis

A sound, healthy and well-maintained financial system is imperative and critical for the efficient running of the business. Rather, a business is started or run based on the books of accounts. Hence, proper care should be taken to maintain and sustain this.

Core framework of the business

The financial system

Banking

Carefully examine the service offerings features and benefits of the product facilities will I get and what will be the charges for each additional perks or offers will I get Will there be a dedicated relationship manager or account manager? In case of issues, how will the issue resolution process work and what will be the turnaround time for this? Will I be able to receive foreign remittances in my account? If yes, what is the procedure to enable it?

Accounting System

Manage all your expenses, revenues, customers, users, salespersons, vendors, invoices, receipts, taxes, compliances, bank accounts, etc. all under one roof

Resource

Resources primarily include accountants and auditors who manage the financial system.

Dos and don'ts for maintaining a "financially healthy" business.

Chapter 8 – Formulation of Business Model

Introduction

Thank you for reading the previous chapters of the entrepreneurship journey. In this chapter, we are going to look at formulating the business model. The business model should be designed for a steady sustained and consistent growth.

Product or Service?

What is your concept? Is it for a product or a service? Any product requires service; however, the converse is not always true. This is the fundamental principle that must be very strongly considered in formulating a sustainable and scalable business model.

For any and every concept that you envisage, ensure that you study the market for your competitor offerings. You need to ensure that you are adding value and being different from your competitors. One strong point is the service aspect to back your product. The customer service or post sales service that you provide to your customers to build relations and maintain them, and wow your prospects in every interaction, will determine your competitiveness and sustainability in the market. The goal will be to get more business by references and word-of-mouth.

Business Model for Products

It is always a good idea to back up your product with a service-based maintenance plan. The product is a one-time revenue generator; the service plan will be a continuous revenue fetcher. Wonderful example is that of a vehicle. To purchase a vehicle, you pay an initial amount. However, with use, the vehicle experiences wear and tear that needs to be addressed. This is where the service centre comes into the picture by the same manufacturer. Every time the vehicle is taken for service, there is a small cost that is paid to the service centre.

Each product that is rolled out, must be constantly innovated and upgraded. To maintain sustainability in the market, the older versions need to be "faded out". In other words, each version of the product should have a life cycle defined. Ideally, it should be from six months to two years. However, the life span would vary from case to case.

Business Model for Services

Service based businesses consist more of project contracts that generally span for a minimum of 6 months to 2 years. However, the duration varies. Services are generally based on creating something from a person's skills, talents and capabilities. These are generally maintenance based or creative in nature. These can be only for a project or for a set of projects under the banner of a service agreement.

It is always a good idea to upsell long term service agreements to your clients in the form of maintenance contracts. The key factor will lie in the way you build and maintain a relation with the client. This will be a deciding factor whether the client will come back to you or not.

Synopsis

It is essential to formulate and devise a business model that is realistic, sustainable, scalable and consistent with provisions for exigencies. Any business model that is designed to spike up, will spiral downwards as well. Exponential growth is good; however, it is not sustainable in the long term. Irrespective of the business model or the product or the service, it is the relationship that you build with your clients that will determine your sustainability and life in the market.

formulating the business model. The business model should be designed for a steady sustained and consistent growth.

Product or Service?

Business Model for Products

The product is a one-time revenue generator.

Each product that is rolled out, must be constantly innovated and upgraded. To maintain sustainability in the market, the older versions need to be "faded out".

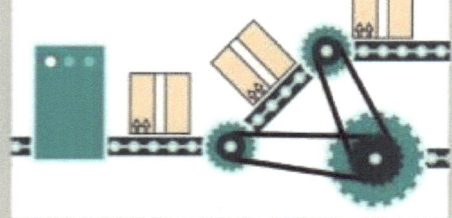

Business Model for Services

The service plan will be a continuous revenue fetcher. Services are generally based on creating something from a person's skills, talents and capabilities.

Chapter 9 – Compliances and Support Functions

Introduction

Thank you for reading the previous chapters of the entrepreneurship journey. In this chapter, we are going to look at a few support functions in the form of internal or external service providers for your core business activity. To efficiently run your business, certain support functions are needed, which may be non-value add activities, however, they are necessary evils. These do not generate revenue; however, they indirectly impact the overall revenue generation process.

In the seventh chapter of this book, we described the different components of the financial system which form the backbone of your business. In this chapter, we will list some of the other components/support functions that form an important part of the company. Some of these tend to be highly overlooked or underestimated, however, they reflect on the company's overall administration.

Compliances – Internal & External

Every business process needs to be documented and rigidly followed. This reflects strongly on the business practices and business ethics. Every company needs to define these in the form of policies and procedures that need to be documented, approved, implemented and practiced and periodically reviewed. This will help to maintain internal compliances and in the efficient functioning of various business processes.

External compliances are in the form of various filings as per prescribed formats that need to be periodically completed and reported to the various governing bodies of the government. These are in the form of various forms, financial statements, tax filings, etc. These need to be regularly completed and filed with the help of a qualified, experienced and practicing Chartered Accountant and/or Company Secretary. This also involves various management reports in different formats.

Human Resources

This consists of recruiting employees, completing the paperwork and other formalities, employee engagement and attrition. Effectively, managing the entire life cycle of employees who are employed in the organization. This requires compliance with labour laws and people who are qualified human resource personnel can take care of these.

Marketing Strategy Consultant

This is a function that can help devise different strategies to increase revenue growth. Although this is an optional function, however, it is growing in importance and prominence. Generally, Founders of a company tend to outsource their marketing activities to agencies which tends to involve a lot of money. This is in turn to acquire customers, enter strategic partnerships, run promo campaigns online and offline, etc.

Synopsis

To summarize, the founders or originators do have a wonderful idea and thought process behind their product and/or service, however, it needs an entire support system to monetize effectively and legally. Hence, there are different types of support systems which may be either internal or external to execute these activities. Some of these are non-value add, however, they are important in their own way and they have their own contribution.

Support functions for your core business activity these do not generate revenue; however, they indirectly impact the revenue generation process.

Compliances – Internal & External

Internal compliances efficient functioning of various business processes.

External compliances various filings as per prescribed formats that need to be periodically completed and reported to the various government and governing bodies.

Human Resources

Recruiting employees, completing the paperwork and other formalities, employee engagement and attrition. Managing the entire life-cycle of employees

Marketing Strategy Consultant

Different strategies to increase revenue growth. Acquire customers, enter strategic partnerships, run promo campaigns online and offline, etc.

Chapter 10 – Creating Brand Awareness

Introduction

Thank you for reading the previous chapters of the entrepreneurship journey. In this chapter, we are going to explore the various commonly adopted strategies to acquire and maintain customers. One key factor to keep in mind is "do not do everything for money". Business will happen, the key is to remain patient and do not run after money.

Attend Entrepreneurship Events

There are plenty of events that are organized by various organizations and groups. Keep an eye out for these and attend these regularly. This will serve a two-fold purpose. First, it will help you learn different aspects about entrepreneurship and second, it will help you network with different people. In such events, share business information in the form of an "elevator pitch", do not pitch to sell your products and/or services. Nobody will make immediate buying decisions. Rather, look to get appointments where collaboration options can be discussed in detail with actionable options. Follow up with a thank you email mentioning your products and services in short.

In the personal meetings, explore various collaboration options in the form of direct and mutual benefits. This will result in more fruitful outcomes. You will also get to meet other entrepreneurs or contacts via referrals. Offer freebies as a vote of thanks. Ensure to maintain good relations by constantly keeping in touch. An occasional phone call or a message (avoid too many forwarded messages).

Social Media Marketing

Social media platforms especially Facebook, LinkedIn, Instagram, Twitter and others are a popular way to get customers for your products and services. The tendency is to write "viral posts" to expand your reach. However, it may not always work. The irony about viral posts is that they get you the numbers in the form of views, likes and comments, however, these do not necessarily convert into business. The key is to have a smaller but more effective reach.

Online and Offline Networking Groups

Look to join meaningful networking groups – either online or offline. There are plenty of such entrepreneurship networking groups online, on various social media platforms and offline as well. Conduct a careful survey of the different groups, attend their meetings as a visitor or as a guest if possible. Meet people who already are members of these groups and get their opinions. Look to join a group or set of groups that have paid memberships. Although free groups are good, however, it is always preferable to join a paid network. The calibre and seriousness of the people in a paid networking group is at a different level altogether.

Synopsis

To summarize, you need to expand your reach via all possible means – online and offline via networking and network marketing. Look to build meaningful relationships via realistic collaborations and affiliations. A strong key don't is "do not do everything for money". They will pay you in the long run.

Do not do everything for money

 Attend Entrepreneurship Events

It will help you learn different aspects about entrepreneurship and it will help you network with different people.

Explore various collaboration options in the form of direct and mutual benefits.

Social Media Marketing

The tendency is to write to expand your reach the key is to have a smaller but more effective reach.

 Online and Offline Networking Groups

Look to join meaningful networking groups – either online or offline. Conduct a careful survey of the different groups, attend their meetings as a visitor if possible.

Chapter 11 – Recognize and Choose your Customer

Introduction

Thank you for reading the previous chapters of the entrepreneurship journey. In this chapter, we are going to understand a bit about the different types of customers and how you need to be choosy about them. One key factor to keep in mind is "choose your customers the way you choose your friends". The money that you earn should be worth the effort.

The Bargaining Type Customer

These are the type of customers that need to be avoided for the below primary reasons. These are more of "loss of business cause" versus "profitable business". These can be politely avoided without price negotiations at the very outset. They will not come back to you. Even if they do, stick to your prices and rates. Do not entertain any kind of special offers or any other package deals with them. They are not worth your time and effort. Do not undermine or underestimate the value of your time and efforts for this type of customers.

1) They will bargain on the price with you without understanding or appreciating the efforts that go behind it.
2) They will not be happy with the product that you give them – no matter how elegant it is.
3) They will not make payments on time and they will make you run behind them.

The Over-Demanding Type of Customers

These are the type of customers who will be ready to pay the price that you ask for, however, they will always look for the additional "value add" – in other words, they will ask for premium features at a lower price without bargaining or negotiating. Do not go all out to satisfy them completely. Draw a line on the service offerings and what is included versus what is not. This is where a documented SOW (Statement of Work) comes in handy. This can always be referred to especially in conflicting or disputed conversations about what is included and what is not.

Customers Who Find Value in Your Offerings

These are the ones you should maintain and cater to. These are the ones who value your service offerings and see value for money. They are the ones who will appreciate your efforts and will remain loyal to you. These are customers who will recommend you and your services to others even if they themselves do not avail of your services. Treasure these customers with special offers and periodic package deals. They will opt for these packages. These are the ones who will take their own time to respond to your quotation, however, their response will always be positive.

Synopsis

To summarize, choose your customers properly and wisely. Your efforts should justify the price that you demand or ask for. Do not cater to all customers as everyone will not find value in your offerings. Do not undervalue yourself to satisfy all your customers, you will not be able to.

Different types of customers and how you need to be choosy about them.

The Bargaining Type Customer

1. They will bargain on the price with you without understanding or appreciating the efforts that go behind it.
2. They will not be happy with the product that you give them – no matter how elegant it is.
3. They will not make payments on time and they will make you run behind them.

The Over-Demanding Type of Customers

Draw a line on the service offerings and what is included versus what is not.

Customers Who Find Value in Your Offerings

who will appreciate your efforts and will remain loyal to you.

Chapter 12 – The Conclusion

Introduction

Thank you for reading the previous chapters of the entrepreneurship journey. This is the concluding chapter of this journey. The intent of this journey was to make aspiring and young entrepreneurs aware of the surrounding activities and to set expectations accordingly. Experienced entrepreneurs can also benefit from this series, especially if they find some useful tips and pointers, which they can implement.

The Beginning

Start the journey by making an informed decision. Weigh the pros and cons of your ideas and career aspirations carefully before embarking on your journey. This is the stage wherein you can identify potential partners who will walk the distance with you in your journey.

Service Providers

Choose your service providers carefully based on several factors – cost is only one of the factors and not the only deciding factor. At various stages, there are various support activities and functions that need to be executed. Do not get caught in the trap of doing them by yourself. Delegate tasks as appropriate and only do work as per your capabilities and potential.

Company Collaterals

Make sure that you have proper collaterals prepared for the company. Logo, visiting cards, letterheads, presentation templates, pitch deck, service offerings, business model (use the business canvas), product or service brochure, etc. These should be designed in a way to reflect the company's brand and value proposition. Use appropriate online and offline materials – website, flyers, banners, product catalogues, service brochures, pamphlets, leaflets, etc.

Investors

It's good to get funding to develop your product and/or services, however, exercise caution while choosing your investor. Do proper background checks on your investors (even if they are a company or a bank or whatever type of entity). Make sure that when the deal is finalized, proper agreements, terms and conditions, etc are in place. Whet the documents through your lawyer if needed. Spend the extra rupee upfront – this will help you save thousands. Remember, "prevention is better than cure".

Target Customers

Choose your customers. Remember, in your company, you make all your selections. You choose your business partner, co-founder, business model, service provider, investor, employees, etc. Customers should not be an exception. You are running your company with a set of products and/or services that have a certain value. You need to value your ideas and not give in and sell it for "cheap". Value your offerings and do smart business. You might not get customers, however, be patient and persistent in your efforts. They will pay you in the long run.

Synopsis

To summarize, entrepreneurship is a journey that requires consistency and persistence in efforts. A sustainable entrepreneur is a person who has "sustainability" in his/her attitude and approach. Think long term and short term as well. You will reap rewards accordingly. For help and further guidance, do feel free to reach me as per my contact info mentioned in the appendix.

to make aspiring and young entrepreneurs aware of the journey

Company Collaterals

Logo, visiting cards, letterheads, presentation templates, pitch deck, service offerings, business model product or service brochure, etc.

The Beginning

Weigh the pros and cons of your ideas and career aspirations carefully before embarking on your journey.

Investors

It's good to get funding to develop your product and/or services, however, exercise caution while choosing your investor.

Service Providers

Choose your service providers carefully based on several factors – cost is only one of the factors and not the only deciding factor.

Target Customers

Choose your customer audience with specific class, age and mindset.

About the Author

Ayaz is an out of the box thinker and loves to look beyond the obvious. He has the uncanny knack of spotting things where people generally overlook or oversee. He is an avid fan of continuous learning and firmly believes that every interaction is a learning experience. Hence, he seeks to learn something new from everyone every day.

During his professional career, he has consistently delivered award-winning performances as an eminent team-player. Often, he has been an unsung hero – delivering performances without hogging the limelight. He has come across many managers with different managing styles and approaches, the good, the bad and the ugly. He has chosen to extract, learn and implement the good from each.

He believes that entrepreneurship is a thought process and a lifestyle that can be adopted by anyone and applied to personal and professional life. He had his stints of entrepreneurship from the early stages of his life. He had learnt a bit about business the old-fashioned way from his father. He had learnt how to manage a distributed setup and different people in different locations.

Amongst one of his earlier ventures was that of an internet café or a cybercafé, which did not give him the returns as he had envisaged. Nevertheless, he had not let his failure bog him down. Rather, he simply moved on to get a job and advance his career. He took all his jobs as learning various aspects of the business, the different sub-entities within the larger umbrella and how they gel together.

Armed with that knowledge and experience, he is currently heading two ventures:

1. **ZANZERIA FAMILY CONSULTANTS (OPC) Pvt Ltd.**
    a. Written and Media Content Development.
    b. Specializing in short text/musical videos.
    c. Tutorial Video Series.
    d. Visual representations – static or graphical.
    e. Personal Finance Management.
    f. Mentoring and Consulting.

   Tag Line: **a written and media content development studio**

   Associated Brand(s):

   - **Artismatic Magnifico** – artistic creativity in its charismatic magnificence.

2. **INMUTATIO CONSULERE Pvt Ltd.**
    a. Business Process Improvement.
    b. Voice of Customer Analysis.
    c. Customer Experience Enhancement Program.
    d. Business Publications.
    e. Leadership and Organizational Development.
    f. Corporate Branding and Communication.

   Tag Line: **re-imagine » re-think » re-engineer**

   Associated Brand(s):

   - **Azimuth** – Customer Driven Initiatives to Improve Business Processes
   - **Chrysalis** – Enhancing Leadership Skills for Effective Change Management
   - **Lexicon** – Redefining Corporate Communications

A bit about his history, he was born and brought up in the Island city of Mumbai where he spent nearly 35 years of his life. He has worked in several companies in different roles and fulfilled different responsibilities as required by the businesses.

The primary strength that Ayaz has is the ability to learn quickly. He has not done too many courses apart from completing his Bachelor's in Automobile Engineering. All his skills have been acquired and polished practically on the job.

Ayaz is straightforward and blunt, which is resented by many. He firmly believes that an initial ugly bluntness is far better than hidden rosy falseness. It is this approach coupled with a never give up attitude and approach that has kept him going through various hardships of life.

He has been approached by many for various reasons. For consulting, mentoring, counselling, advice, business partnerships, business projects, to name a few. He was involved in founding and setting up a few companies from which he has moved out for various reasons (personal and professional).

Although not very good at marketing or selling, he has an uncanny knack of striking good conversations even with little knowledge of the topic. He believes that learning is a never-ending process that never stops at any age or designation. Another reason for being open to learning is his belief in change is constant. Change is inevitable and will happen. Hence, rather than resist change, welcome it with open arms.

Ayaz does not believe in money making gimmicks or get rich quick schemes. Rather he prefers to take the slow and steady consistent and sustainable approach for making money. He has tried this approach with his knowledge of share trading which is paying him rich dividends.

Ayaz can be reached on various social media platforms and via contact info as listed in the appendix. Alternately, the simplest way is to type "Ayaz Zanzeria" in google search to find him and ways to contact him.

Appendix

The simplest way is to type "Ayaz Zanzeria" in google search. The search results will give a listing of all his websites, social media profiles and other listings on other websites. Specific contact info is as below.

Company Websites

- ❖ https://thezanzeriafamily.com
- ❖ https://artismatic.gallery
- ❖ https://inmutatio.com

Personal Websites

- ❖ https://ayazzanzeria.page
- ❖ https://thejanz.rocks

Professional Contact

- ❖ ayaz@thezanzeriafamily.com
- ❖ ayaz@inmutatio.com
- ❖ Call/Text/WhatsApp: +91 80955 03465 / +91 63606 17899
- ❖ Skype: ayaz.zanzeria / ayaz@thezanzeriafamily.com

Personal Contact

- ❖ hi@ayazzanzeria.page
- ❖ ayaz@thejanz.rocks
- ❖ ayaz.zanzeria@hotmail.com
- ❖ ayazzanzeria@gmail.com

www.ingramcontent.com/pod-product-compliance
Lightning Source LLC
Chambersburg PA
CBHW040247220526
45473CB00001B/403